THE
BOOK
OF THE
FEW

A Secular
Interpretation
of Biblical Creation

BY HARRY WALTER MOSS, SR.

EDITED BY STEVE MOSS

NEW TIMES PRESS
JOHN DANIEL AND COMPANY

THE BOOK OF THE FEW

New Times Press
197 Santa Rosa St.,
San Luis Obispo, Calif. 93405
805-546-8208
mail@newtimes-slo.com

Distributed to the trade by
Daniel & Daniel, Publishers, Inc.,
Post Office Box 21922, Santa Barbara, CA 93121

Editor and Project Director: Steve Moss
Design direction by Steve Moss and Alex Zuniga
Design by Alex Zuniga
Proofreading by Diane DeRushia Urbani

*Love and gratitude is extended to Elizabeth Donnellan Moss,
as well as to June Reno Moss and Harry, Kioren, Francis, Alice,
and Laura Moss. Their contribution to the life of the author
was immeasurable and beyond expression.*

Library of Congress Cataloging-in-Publication Data

Moss, Harry Walter. 1913-1989
  The book of the few: a secular interpretation of biblical
creation / by Harry Walter Moss, Sr. ; [editor and project
director, Steve Moss].
    p. cm.
  Contains text of Gen. 2:5-3:24, New English Bible.
  ISBN 1-880284-25-1
  1. Creation 2. Creation—Biblical teaching. 3. Bible. O.T.
Genesis II, 5-III, 24—Criticism, interpretation, etc. I Moss,
Steve, 1948- . II Bible. O.T. Genesis II, 5-III, 24. English.
New English. 1997. III. Title.
BS651.M79   1997
222' . 1106—DC21   96-44023
                                                     CIP

Published in the United States of America
First Edition

CONTENTS

INTRODUCTION

This manuscript was discovered by accident. Shortly after our father's death, we divided his few personal effects among us and I soon found myself bringing home a cardboard box full of his writings that we had found in his home office. These were Dad's legal tablets, each one filled with his elegant handwriting that, together, spanned some 60 years of personal reminiscence.

Much of what Dad had written dealt with his boyhood in Illinois, his years of practicing law, and various ruminations on historical and contemporary events. Being his son, I found them fascinating. There I was holding a written record of my father's thoughts, penned in his own hand, to pass on to his descendants. Few among us have such a treasure.

Why Dad wrote, I don't know. I think he simply enjoyed both the discipline and the satisfaction of the moment, for he never spoke of publishing anything. The sight of him at home writing in those long, yellow legal pads was familiar to the family, as common as his reading the morning newspaper.

During the weeks that followed, I spent most of my time reading through his writings. Eventually, I decided that much of it should be published, if not for a wider audience, then at least for his friends and family.

In the course of organizing the manuscript of his memoirs, the last thing I looked at was a folder at the bottom of the pile, which at first seemed filled with nothing but scrap papers, and which I was prepared to discard. On the folder's tab, Dad had written, "The Book of the Few." Inside it were many versions of an essay that apparently never met with his satisfaction.

If that was the case, I think he was being overly modest. The manuscript was almost finished, after all. Yes, it was a puzzle, but it just needed someone to put the pieces together. What luck. I was an editor. And I liked puzzles. The result is the book you're holding in your hands.

But the biggest puzzle to me is that Dad never spoke about the central idea in "The Book of the Few." This was odd because, being a lawyer by profession and an historian by inclination, he enjoyed talking about all manner of historical, religious, and contemporary affairs. He didn't keep things to himself.

But this unusual interpretation of Genesis that he'd cast aside unfinished in that folder had no connection with anything I'd ever heard him discuss. Reading it was as new to me as it will be to you.

Dad knew the Bible better than most ministers. He'd studied it for many years and considered it a book of great learning. But he had little patience with those who attempted to use it for their own self-aggrandizement or to keep others in ignorance.

He was not a religious man in any traditional sense of the word, but he did have a belief in immortality that was very simple.

Dad believed that knowledge was vital to living a full life, that it was the one thing that enlarged it and gave it richness. He also believed that if he imparted knowledge to another person, they would then know something they'd not known before and that this would influence their life in a positive way. They, in turn, would eventually pass the knowledge on to someone else, and so on. In this manner, Dad thought, he would live forever.

"The Book of the Few" is a compassionate view

of the human condition, and of why we must for-ever seek knowledge and share it. It is the result of a logical mind attempting to make sense of both history and faith, while being true to both.

It is a secular view of Biblical creation that offers readers a cogent, non-religious interpretation of one of the world's most famous stories, while retaining the kind of uplifting quality usually asso-ciated only with religious beliefs.

I think this was Dad's intent, even though he evi-dently believed he'd failed to convey the knowledge and wisdom he'd left unfinished in a folder at the bottom of a cardboard box.

But he was wrong; he didn't fail at all. Instead, he succeeded at creating a transcendent work of great originality that shows readers not only his unique view of mankind's place on this Earth, gleaned from his own years of thoughtful study, but something more.

He also succeeded at presenting the world with a compelling argument that the ancient Biblical text of Genesis was not written to instill guilt and fear, but to offer hope and reason in an uncertain world.

I think Dad would be pleased to know that you're about to read it, and that this small piece of knowledge is being passed on.

Steve Moss

THE
BOOK
OF THE
FEW

There is a beautiful story hidden in the Book of Genesis.

Most people have heard it, and I'm sure you have too. It's the story of Adam and Eve, a familiar tale that was written to illustrate a great truth.

Unfortunately, its true meaning has been lost.

This is due in large part to the many crude additions made to the story since it was first written, bits of text inserted by those who weren't really interested in its truth or beauty.

A little study, however, will reveal its original intent.

First, let me tell you what the story of Adam and Eve is not.

It is not intended to convince you that you should believe in God or the Bible. It is not about original sin or the Fall of Man, which so many have used to make so many others feel guilty.

Instead, it is a philosopher's explanation of the nature of mankind and our place in the world.

It is an allegory—a fiction—and I'm certain it was written as such. Whoever first told it back in the early days of recorded history knew exactly what he was writing and why. The writer was creating a symbolic tale, never intending it to be taken literally.

When stripped of its clutter, the story is a simple way of expressing a great idea.

Getting rid of this extraneous material is the first task. What follows in these pages is my attempt to do so through thoughtful editing. What I have done is to remove certain passages from the scripture. If the reader will indulge me—and not judge me blasphemous for my efforts—I will soon explain why. Then I will comment on the remaining text to reveal its essential purpose.

Here, then, is the story of Adam and Eve as it appears in the New English Bible under the heading, "The Beginnings of History." I could have chosen any of the many different Bibles that have been published over the centuries, because all of them have various extraneous material that was added to them later. But this one will do.

In the New English Bible, the story of God creating Adam and Eve and their expulsion from the Garden of Eden begins in Chapter 2 of Genesis with Verse 5, and ends with Verse 24 in Chapter 3. I've made no changes to the text. I've merely underlined the irrelevant and distracting material that hides the real story.

It may be easier for some people to read the scripture on the following pages straight through and ignore my underlined edits entirely, then read it again and skip over the excised sections before reading my comments. Others may find it simpler to first read my edited version in its entirety, then refer back to the original text to see what I have deleted.

2

5 When the Lord God made earth and heaven, there was neither shrub nor plant growing wild upon the earth <u>because the Lord God had sent no rain on the earth;</u> nor was

6 there any man to till the ground. <u>A flood used to rise out of the earth and water all the surface of the ground.</u>

7 Then the Lord God formed a man from the dust of the ground and breathed into his nostrils the breath of life. Thus the man became a living creature.

8 Then the Lord God planted a garden in Eden away to the east and there he put the man whom he had formed.

9 The Lord God made trees spring from the ground, all trees pleasant to look at and good for food; and in the garden he set the Tree of Life and the Tree of Knowledge of good and evil.

10 There was a river flowing from Eden to water the garden, and when it left the garden

11 it branched into four streams. The name of the first is Pishon; that is the river which encircles all the land of Havilah, where the

12 gold is. The gold of that land is good; bdellium and cornelians are also to be found there.

13 The name of the second river is Gihon; this is the one which encircles all the land of Cush.

14 The name of the third is Tigris; this is the river which runs east of Asshur. The fourth river is Euphrates.

15 The Lord God took the man and put him in the garden of Eden to till it and care for it.

16 He told the man, "You may eat from every tree in the garden, but not from the Tree of

17 Knowledge of good and evil; for on that day you eat from it, you will surely die."

18 Then the Lord God said, "It is not good for the man to be alone. I will provide a partner for him."

19 <u>So God formed out of the ground all the wild animals and all the birds of heaven. He brought them to the man to see what he would call them, and whatever the man called each living creature, that was its name.</u>

20 <u>Thus the man gave names to all cattle, to the birds of heaven, and to every wild animal. But for the man himself, no partner</u>

21 <u>had yet been found.</u> And so the Lord God put the man into a trance, and while he slept, he took one of his ribs and closed the

22 flesh over the place. The Lord God then built up the rib, which he had taken out of the man, into a woman. He brought her to the man.

23 <u>And the man said, "Now this, at last, bone from my bones, flesh from my flesh, this shall be called woman, for from man was</u>

24 <u>this taken." That is why a man leaves his father and mother, and is united to his wife, and the two become one flesh.</u>

25 Now they were both naked, the man and

his wife, but they had no feeling of shame towards one another.

3

The serpent was more crafty than any wild creature that the Lord God had made. He said to the woman, "Is it true that God has forbidden you to eat from the tree in the garden?" The woman answered the serpent, "We may eat the fruit of any tree in the garden, except for the tree in the middle of the garden; God has forbidden us either to eat or to touch the fruit of that; if we do, we shall die." The serpent said, "Of course you will not die. God knows that as soon as you eat it, your eyes will be opened and you will be like gods, knowing both good and evil." When the woman saw that the fruit of the tree was good to eat, and that it was pleasing to the eye and tempting to contemplate, she took some and ate it. She also

7 gave her husband some and he ate it. Then the eyes of both of them were opened and they discovered that they were naked; so they stitched fig leaves together and made themselves loincloths.

8 The man and his wife heard the sounds of the Lord God walking in the garden at the time of the evening breeze and hid from the Lord God among the trees of the garden.

9 But the Lord God called to the man and said to him, "Where are you?" He replied, "I heard the sound as you were walking in the garden, and I was afraid because I was

11 naked, and I hid myself." God answered, "Who told you that you were naked? Have you eaten from the tree from which I've

12 forbade you?" The man said, "The woman you gave me for a companion, she gave me

13 fruit from the tree and I ate it." Then the Lord God said to the woman, "What is this

14 that you have done?" The woman said,

"The serpent tricked me, and I ate." Then the Lord God said <u>to the serpent: "Because you have done this, you are accursed more than all cattle and all wild creatures. On your belly you will crawl, and dust you</u>

15 <u>shall eat all the days of your life. I will put enmity between you and the woman, between your brood and hers. They shall strike at your head, and you shall strike at their heel."</u>

16 <u>To the woman he said, "I will increase your labour and your groaning, and in labour you shall bear children. You shall be eager for your husband, and he shall be your</u>

17 <u>master." To the man he said, "Because you have eaten from the tree which I forbade you, accursed shall be the ground on your account. With labour you shall win your</u>

18 <u>food from it all the days of your life. It will grow thorns and thistles for you, none but</u>

19 <u>plants for you to eat. You shall gain your</u>

bread by the sweat of your brow until you return to the ground; for from it you were

20 taken. Dust you are, to dust you shall return." The man called his wife Eve because she was the mother of all who live.

21 The Lord God made tunics of skins for Adam and his wife and clothed them. He

22 said, "The man has become like one of us, knowing good and evil; what if he now reaches out his hand and takes fruit from

23 the Tree of Life also, and lives forever?" So the Lord God drove him out of the garden of Eden to till the ground from which he had been taken.

24 He cast him out, and to the east of the garden of Eden he stationed the cherubim and a sword whirling and flashing to guard the way to the Tree of Life.

The first thing I've deleted is the section in Verse 5 about there being no rain. It's apparent that someone added that later; perhaps it was inserted by a transcriber who wanted to remind us of God's awesome power in our daily life, and how he might withhold his largess if we do not obey Him. I don't know.

What I do know is that it has nothing to do with the story, but merely distracts. If you leave it out, you can see how the sentence easily and naturally connects from "wild upon the earth" to "nor was there any man." Take a moment and reread it without the phrase "because the Lord God had sent no rain on the earth," and I think you'll see what I mean.

The same is true of Verse 6, which should also be deleted: "A flood used to rise out of the earth and water all the surface of the ground." This sentence is even more out of place than my first example; you can actually feel its abruptness cutting off the narrative flow. It is another distraction that serves no purpose other than to perhaps be awesome and frightening.

Again, the story moves more naturally from one idea to the next without it.

❧

Verses 10 through 14 describing the names of various rivers in Eden also appear to have been added later, no doubt by someone trying to describe the physical location of the garden. They may have been hoping to give the story some basis in fact in order to answer skeptics who might ask, "So, where was this garden?"

Whoever added this paragraph failed to recognize Genesis as the allegory it's intended to be. They thought the garden needed a real location, when it doesn't. The paragraph merely adds more distraction and confusion; it sounds like a geography lesson.

Again, when you read the text without it, you'll sense the natural rhythm of the words from the paragraph preceding it— Verse 9—ending with "Tree of Knowledge of good and evil" to the beginning of Verse

THE BOOK OF THE FEW

15, starting with the words, "The Lord God took the man..."

Verses 19 through 20 should also be omitted. God says that he will provide a partner for Adam, and then goes off creating animals for Adam to name. This makes no sense. After all, if God said he was going to provide a partner, that is exactly what he would do next. He wouldn't start making turtles and badgers and seagulls hoping to perhaps stumble upon something Adam might like.

I believe this section was added by someone who was again hoping to make things seem logical. They had God create all the world's animals just in case skeptics wondered why the story didn't explain where the birds and the beasts of the field came from.

If you just skip this section and pick the narrative up again where God puts Adam into a trance, the story is more coherent and sensible.

Then, farther down after God creates woman, Verse 22 should end with "and he brought her to the man," and skip to "Now they were both naked" in Verse 25. Omit

Adam's speech in Verse 23 through Verse 24. Besides breaking the story's continuity, it sounds pompous and silly.

The section in Verse 24 that talks about a man leaving his parents is more over-explaining by someone who thinks the reader is always in need of answers to every little thing. It, too, is unnecessary and out of place.

If you delete it, you'll note the natural transition as you read, "He brought her to the man" (Verse 22) and then take up the story again at Verse 25 with, "Now they were both naked, the man and his wife, but they had no feelings of shame towards one another."

I realize that all of this skipping over verses must seem tedious, but I assure you that I have a point to make if you'll just bear with me a moment more.

Now let us look at Chapter 3.

As Chapter 3 begins, the narrative is clear and things are fine through almost all of Verse 14. But then we run into more distractions.

I'm referring to Verse 14 through Verse

19, where God gives a speech to the serpent, then to Eve, and then to Adam. This is little more than a mighty scolding from the Almighty, and serves as yet another example of admonishments inserted by someone hoping to instill fear through holy wrath. Omit them.

Verses 20 and 21 are superfluous as well. Verse 20 is simply out of place; Adam would have had a name for Eve long before it's mentioned here—they had been living together in the garden for a long time, after all. God making tunics in Verse 20 sounds prudish and very un-Godlike. If you skip all that, the end of Verse 14 ("Then the Lord God said...") connects to Verse 22 with God's pronouncement that "The man has become like one of us, knowing good and evil."

Chapter 3 ends with Verse 24 when God banishes Adam and Eve from the garden of Eden, where he stations a "cherubim and a sword whirling and flashing to guard the way to the Tree of Life."

Here, then, on the following pages is the edited scripture. I'm certain it is much closer to the way the Book of Genesis was originally written.

When the Lord God made earth and heaven, there was neither shrub nor plant growing wild upon the earth, nor was there any man to till the ground. Then the Lord God formed a man from the dust of the ground and breathed into his nostrils the breath of life. Thus the man became a living creature.

Then the Lord God planted a garden in Eden away to the east and there he put the man whom he had formed. The Lord God made trees spring from the ground, all trees pleasant to look at and good for food; and in the middle of the garden he set the Tree of Life and the Tree of Knowledge of good and evil.

The Lord God took the man and put him in the garden of Eden to till it and care for it.

He told the man, "You may eat from every tree in the garden, but not from the Tree of Knowledge of good and evil; for on that day you eat from it, you will surely die."

Then the Lord God said, "It is not good for the man to be alone. I will provide a partner for him." And so the Lord God put the man into a trance, and while he slept, he took one of his ribs and closed the flesh over the place. The Lord God then built up the rib, which he had taken out of the man, into a woman. He brought her to the man. Now they were both naked, the man and his wife, but they had no feeling of shame towards one another.

The serpent was more crafty than any wild creature that the Lord God had made. He said to the woman, "Is it true that God has forbidden you to eat from the tree in the garden?" The woman answered the serpent, "We may eat the fruit of any tree in the garden, except for the tree in the middle of the garden; God has forbidden us either to eat or to touch the fruit of that; if we do, we shall die." The serpent said, "Of course you will not die. God knows that as soon as you eat it, your eyes will be opened and you will be like gods, knowing both good and evil."

When the woman saw that the fruit of the tree was good to eat, and that it was pleasing to the eye and tempting to contemplate, she took some and ate it. She also gave her husband some and he ate it. Then the eyes of both of them were opened and they discovered that they were naked; so they stitched fig leaves together and made themselves loincloths.

The man and his wife heard the sounds of the Lord God walking in the garden at the time of the evening breeze and hid from the Lord God among the trees of the garden. But the Lord God called to the man and said to him, "Where are you?" He replied, "I

heard the sound as you were walking in the garden, and I was afraid because I was naked, and I hid myself." God answered, "Who told you that you were naked? Have you eaten from the tree which I've forbade you?" The man said, "The woman you gave me for a companion, she gave me fruit from the tree and I ate it." Then the Lord God said to the woman, "What is this that you have done?" The woman said, "The serpent tricked me, and I ate."

Then the Lord God said, "The man has become like one of us, knowing good and evil; what if he now reaches out his hand and takes fruit from the Tree of Life also, and lives forever?" So the Lord God drove him out of the garden of Eden to till the ground from which he had been taken. He cast him out, and to the east of the garden of Eden he stationed the cherubim and a sword whirling and flashing to guard the way to the Tree of Life.

As you can see, the narrative now flows seamlessly, as if being told by a single narrator instead of a committee. The extraneous details and moral pronouncements that I've deleted brought abrupt changes to the narration and did nothing but obscure it.

Without them, we can now begin to study the true meaning of the scripture.

So what is the point of the story? What is the writer trying to tell us?

I believe that when the excess passages are stripped away, it becomes clear that the main purpose of the text is to explain why, of all animals, we humans are different—and why we should not be fearful or ashamed of this difference.

God told Adam and Eve that they "may eat from every tree in the garden." This is what all the other creatures of the Earth do, too. They partake of life—eating from every tree in the garden—then they grow, propagate, and die. It is the natural, observable cycle of life.

But only man was forbidden to eat from

the Tree of Knowledge. He disobeyed. Because of this, he is unique. The Book of Genesis is explaining our separateness from nature even though we remain connected to it.

We are different, says Genesis, because our eyes have been opened to knowledge.

All creatures of the Earth, from the tiniest insects to the largest beasts, continue the life cycle in ignorance. They know not why they exist, nor do they care. They simply are. But Adam and Eve bit into that fruit and changed into something very different; something not quite animal any longer, and yet not quite God.

The Tree of Knowledge, of course, is not intended to be a real tree; it's a symbol used to show us how Adam and Eve got an education. The writer doesn't know why we alone have the ability to learn; he only knows that it's true. That is the main point of the allegory, one of the truths explained.

Adam and Eve both eat of the tree, but they don't die immediately from poisoned fruit, even though God tells them, "On the day you eat of it, you will surely die." A child upon hearing this for the first time would naturally ask, "But I thought God said they'd die

if they did that." This is another indication that the story was intended to be taken symbolically, not literally.

What Adam and Eve acquired after eating the forbidden fruit was not just knowledge of their nakedness, but of the short time they have on this Earth—that, yes, someday they will surely die.

This is just another way of describing man's awareness of his own mortality, which is also part of his separateness. We are the only animal, after all, that understands our days upon this Earth are limited. This gives us some of our sorrow, but all of our humanity.

Again, it is knowledge and self-awareness that allow us this understanding, because they are what separate us from all other creatures.

❦

The message in Genesis is simple: Only mankind can learn because only mankind was given the opportunity to seek knowledge.

Having a little knowledge—that is, knowing good and evil and the difference between them—is the flint that lights the road to further learning.

Adam and Eve acquired knowledge and self-awareness, two things that, until their

eyes were opened, only God possessed.

You've heard God referred to as "the All-knowing." This is a reasonable idea; after all, whatever power created the universe must surely know everything there is to know. It would have to. How else could galaxies have been spun from nothingness?

The author of Genesis no doubt had a different idea of the Creator than I do. But he clearly believed that He is the sum of all knowledge. The scripture suggests that whatever mankind doesn't know or understand, God certainly does.

It also suggests that the more we learn, the more godlike we will become. With knowledge comes the ability to create, just as the creator of the universe has done. The more knowledge we have, the more we can achieve. As the serpent tells Adam and Eve, "Your eyes will be opened and you will be like gods, knowing good and evil."

This is another of the truths revealed.

❧

But there's just one problem with mankind becoming like the Almighty, and Genesis addresses this, too.

Even if we study all our lives and learn everything we can, our knowledge will always be limited because we have but one lifetime, far too brief a span to ever understand very much about the world and all its complexities.

Adam and Eve know the solution to this dilemma: After eating from the Tree of Knowledge, they must next eat from the Tree of Life so they can live forever and learn everything. If they could do this, the centuries would pass and, being immortal, their knowledge would keep growing. So would yours and mine, since we would be the children of immortals.

Eventually, mankind would catch up to God; like God, we too would one day become all-knowing.

But God has kept this from happening, the story tells us. Adam and Eve didn't listen the first time—they took the fruit and their eyes were opened to knowledge.

God then says, "The man has become like one of us, knowing good and evil; what if he now reaches out his hand and takes fruit from the Tree of Life also, and lives forever?"

The first tree has been robbed; now the second one is within easy reach.

But God will not be tricked again. He banishes Adam and Eve from the garden. This time, he takes no chances—he places a fiery guard in front of the Tree of Life so mankind can never eat from it and never live long enough to become like Him. Death will always end our quest to know more about the world.

And so it does. We join the great cycle of birth and extinction, but with a self-awareness beyond that of any other creature and a natural thirst for knowledge that is always cut short by death.

I believe the writer of Genesis was giving words to something so many of us already sense: that to be human is to be adrift somewhere between two worlds, with nature behind us from whence we came, and the loftiness of creation far ahead of us, forever unattainable.

To be part of either would bring great serenity—to be joined completely to the great kaleidoscope of blissfully ignorant life, unconscious of our own mortality, or to be somewhere high above it, immortal, godlike, and all-knowing.

But we are neither, says Genesis. We cannot go back. We can only go forward.

We ate of the Tree of Knowledge, which started us on our journey, but not of the Tree of Life, which would have allowed us to travel forever. And this, the story tells us, is our torment.

So if you take the Book of Genesis as an allegory, a tale that is not intended to make us fearful of the Creator and His wrath, but instead is trying to explain why we are unique creatures with qualities unlike those of any others, you will understand the great truth the writer is attempting to convey.

When read as an allegory, then, "God" is not presented as something we're to comprehend. In the context of Genesis, He is not a literal apparition. His behavior toward Adam and Eve is used allegorically to explain the human condition.

Where did the world come from? Why does mankind exist? These are profound questions that have always been with us. I do not have the answers. And I don't know whether the author of Genesis was really trying to find them.

The only thing knowable, the writer tells us, is that the world does exist, that we are indeed a part of it, and—most important— that we alone of all Earth's creatures ask such questions.

We have abilities far beyond those of our animal brethren and something akin to those of our maker, says Genesis. We build cities and paint paintings and gaze up at the stars in wonderment. We are different. We have eaten from the Tree of Knowledge and our eyes have been opened.

The only thing keeping us from becoming truly godlike in our quest for knowledge is the curse of mortality imposed on us so long ago by the mysterious creator of all things.

I have never read of anyone giving the meaning of Genesis I've just outlined, and yet it seems impossible to me that others have not done so.

I realize that this interpretation could not be accepted by religious authorities because it is too open-ended; it gives freedom to people by showing them why they must seek knowledge instead of simple answers.

Such an approach is very dangerous to those who have their own power to protect and followers to instruct.

Instead, the concept of original sin was favored by many religious leaders because it

gave them influence over their believers. And, to be fair, probably also because their followers wanted to believe so that they might find succor in a hostile world.

The rationale for original sin fits in neatly here; why it evolved as a common interpretation of the story is perfectly understandable.

Having knowledge of good and evil, after all, means knowing the difference between right and wrong. Since we cannot always be right, we must sometimes be wrong. It follows, then, that at times we must therefore "sin"; that is, we will choose wrong over right.

But the only way we can be held accountable for our wrong choices is if we know the difference. We would not punish an animal for wrongdoing when it has no concept of its decisions or the results of its actions. That would be cruel and foolish. The only way to justify punishment is to first determine this awareness. Genesis explains how we gained our ability to make these choices.

Interpreting the story as the Fall of Man is understandable, too. Possessing awareness of one's own existence brings with it internal conflict. When compared to the natural state of all other creatures, many have seen the result of this awareness as a discontinuity of some sort, a fall from grace. Ignorance, we're reminded, is indeed bliss.

Whether we have "sinned" is for others to determine. It is not my concern here. What I do know is that we have indeed eaten from the tree.

It seems to me, then, that no matter how one interprets Genesis, it's difficult not to acknowledge that the central purpose of the scripture is to explain our unique ability as human beings to learn.

Others who interpret the text as proof of original sin or mankind's fall from grace are certainly entitled to their opinions, but I have no use for them. I do not know conclusively whether they are right or wrong.

I only know that, yes, there are those whose candle is brighter than mine, but it is still a candle in overwhelming darkness.

If I have learned anything, it is that there is but one god, and His name is Knowledge. This is what I believe.

He has but one commandment: Get the facts.

I refer to him as "He," but only for convenience. My god has no gender and no race,

no holy places or magic stones. He cannot be moved by prayer, or placated with gifts of gold or fatted calves.

My god takes nothing from you. He only gives. He is the universe with all its history. He is everything that ever was or will be. But like all gods, my god of knowledge remains a mystery.

One thing is not a mystery, however: We are human and we want to know more. This quest for knowledge remains mankind's greatest passion.

❧

A few other thoughts about knowledge. Remember that it is never static; it is always changing. It is not a thing, but a process. It does not create fear. Fear comes only from ignorance, for there is no such thing as "evil" knowledge. All of it is good. What people do with the knowledge they acquire is the great test.

As for faith, I do not mean to belittle it. I think it is important too, because faith is also a form of learning, although a childlike one. At the start of life, children need faith because they have nothing else from which to form an understanding of the world into which they've been born; children must trust their parents and teachers, for these instructors are all they know.

In the beginning, then, faith can be a good teacher. But the student's own experience in life and increasing knowledge eventually make this kind of faith not only unnecessary, but undesirable. Some people are always children.

Thomas Jefferson's statement that "all men are created equal" is repeated so often that it is in danger of losing its meaning. It simply means that all of us are created equally ignorant. When we are born, we know nothing about life, no matter how rich or poor we might be, no matter what our lineage or race. At that moment—and at that moment only—we are all truly equal.

If we are to survive and prosper, then, we must fill our heads with knowledge, for it is the only thing we have going for us. We have no claws like the lion or great speed like the gazelle to outrun the lion. We have only our ability to learn.

That is the message of the scripture. Some of us know what to do with knowledge once we have it. Some of us do not.

❦

I assure you that valuing knowledge and forever seeking it will always bring rewards.

But it will also bring much loneliness. This is another truth that the story in Genesis is attempting to convey.

Because if you decide to seek knowledge, you will become one of the few. Like Adam and Eve, you will become an outcast; you will have left the garden, venturing into the unknown.

And, as one of the few, you won't be liked very much by those who place little trust in that strange god of yours who is always changing and reinventing Himself as new facts are added.

So be courageous in your search. Take pride in those who hate or envy you. And get used to it.

One more thing: Always remember the prayer to the god of Knowledge. It is simple to utter and it goes like this: "I don't know."

It's easy to say, so say it often and you will learn forever. Never forget that being able to say it is the beginning of all knowledge.

And may God be with you always. Δ

ADDENDUM

I have spoken here about how the Bible has changed over time. Here is perhaps a clearer example of what I mean.

Consider the following translations of Proverbs 17, Verse 8, from seven different Bibles. Their transcriptions took place at different times over the course of history. As you can see, those who made the various copies and translations brought along their own thoughts and prejudices when they put quill to parchment.

The effect is somewhat similar to how a rumor evolves, with its content mutating little by little as it moves from one person to the next. Note how the words change within the same verse simply because they were written down by different individuals during different eras.

PROVERBS 17, VERSE 8

PILGRIM EDITION, KING JAMES VERSION

—

"A gift is as a precious stone in the eyes of him that hath it; whithersoever it turneth, it prospereth."

THE JERUSALEM BIBLE

—

"A gift works like a talisman for him who gives it; he prospers whichever way he turns."

THE NEW WORLD BIBLE

—

"The gift is a stone winning favor in the eyes of its grand owner. Everywhere that he turns he has success."

REVISED STANDARD VERSION

—

"A bribe is like a magic stone
in the eyes of him who gives it;
wherever he turns, he prospers."

NEW ENGLISH VERSION

—

"He who offers a bribe
finds it works like a charm;
he prospers in all he undertakes."

THE GOOD NEWS BIBLE

—

"Some people think
a bribe works like magic;
they believe it can do anything."

THE LIVING BIBLE

—

"A bribe works like magic.
Whoever uses it will prosper."
(This version has a footnote that reads:
"This is a fact, but not to be encouraged.")

I think it is clear from these examples the distinct differences found in the scripture due to people bringing their own values to the text they are translating and transcribing. The last one has mutated so much that it elicits an offstage comment by a publisher who was apparently concerned that petty corruption might spread through Bible reading.

This is but one example. Any document that has been copied by hand and recopied again—and then again and again—down through the centuries will suffer the same fate. The Bible is certainly no exception.

Please do not misunderstand me here. I am not suggesting that the Bible is filled with lies. On the contrary, it is a work of great wisdom, one of the most astonishing books ever written.

I am merely saying that, like all things, if the Bible is to be fully appreciated—and fully understood—it must be approached with knowledge.

Harry Walter Moss, Sr.

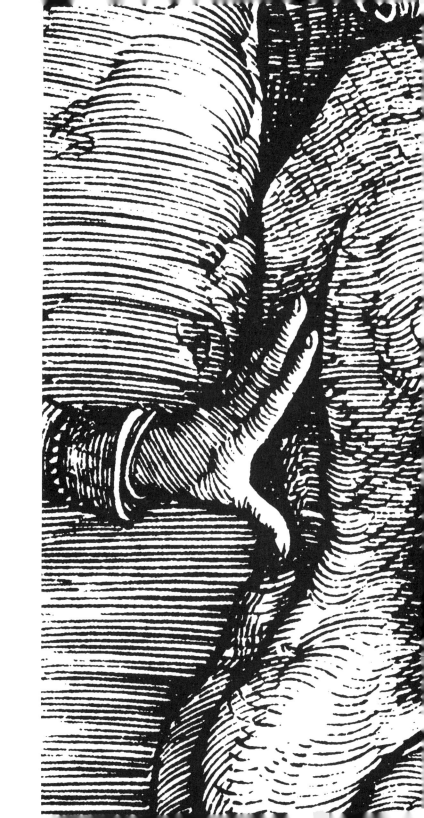

Harry Walter Moss was born on July 16, 1913, in Anna, Illinois.

He received his bachelor's degree in history from Southern Illinois University at Carbondale in 1934, and graduated from the University of Southern California Law School in 1938. He was admitted to the California State Bar that same year.

He practiced law in Imperial and San Diego counties prior to his enlistment in the United States Army, where he served from 1942 to 1946, attaining the rank of first lieutenant.

Following the war, he returned to California and became a deputy district attorney with the Riverside County District Attorney's Office before entering private practice. During his career as an attorney, he specialized in both civil and criminal law, representing clients in the state and federal courts.

He always considered himself to be a professional problem solver, handling whatever difficulties the general public might find itself in—something it always managed to do—so he was kept busy.

Mr. Moss' writings have been published posthumously by The Texas Criminal Defense Lawyers Association, Dayton Bar Briefs, For the Defense, New Times, and The Wall Street Journal.

He died in Ventura, Calif., on April 19, 1989.

DESIGN DIRECTION BY
STEVE MOSS AND ALEX ZUNIGA

ART DIRECTION BY ALEX ZUNIGA

TYPESET IN STEMPEL GARAMOND AND
WOODTYPE ORNAMENTS
BY ADOBE SYSTEMS INCORPORATED